Broken Wing

by

Adam Tod Leverton

Part One: Broken Wing

Part Two: Sex and Love

Part Four: Landscapes

Yesterday

there are the screams
and there's the disgust
she looks so good
she's a God girl
she's abrupt and impolite
she's everything I don't have
what do you have?
illumination delight devotion
now's your chance
a passing glance
a clasped hand
will she succumb to this grazing seduction?
but o heaven is for
the vacillators and the uncertain
I see her across a crowded room
she's arrogant and pompous
I wish I could crush her
vacuous head with a rock or something
a classic example of hating
something you desire for desiring it
o I could kill her
out out damn spot
the blood would never come off
guilt prone for even thinking about it
do you ever want things desire things?
I'm good and godly and cynical

I get what I want and then I don't want it anymore
like the girl I seduced
like the rum I drank
like the pot I smoked
and the hangover after
but there she is
standing pretty
embathed in blue a solemn hue
and the sphere rotates
and she stands there
embathed in blue
a solemn hue.

I found a creature of beautiful burning

I found a creature of beautiful burning

in a thousand guises
hid

and then
you awake me
discovery
eyes breasts arms legs

and your touch feels like a thousand hands
and your warmth feels like a thousand suns
you are a thing of thousands.

Morning

in the morning
you wake up
yawn and smile
gather up your things
of sleeping
and toss them aside
as if shrugging off
the rumour of death

Away, Come

Away, come.
To this place,
this land.
Trace lines
in my empty,
open hand.

by the river

walking
beside a river
I throw away the leaves
I gathered up
lose my balance
and slip into your arms.

Gloom

You’re lost.
Somewhere in the dark.
Wait. I'll search.
Discover. Kiss. Scald.
With the soft flame tongue
(of my yearning).

You

I dreamt of you
between the broken sleep
of longing
of pining
and you.

and summer's yearning comes up
all green and growing and decadent
through the quilt
of the leaves
of the sun
of the sky
this morning
all fatigue and a smile
bitter, but not yet broken.

I Could Walk

I could walk around
in the rain and get wet
the smiles of a stranger
I could dawdle uselessly
read stupid books
I could wait until nightfall
seduce you, tempt you.

If Two By Fire

The city is burning.
Come flee with me to the hills.
The Greeks have burst
from the belly of their great horse.

This is another poem
about the ruin of our universe.
They'll char the city
make it black and drag
that hag Helen back.

There are lines on her face now,
almost as if the entire war
had been scratched out in flesh.

This is the war of the old,
let Troy burn with a whimper.
Let's go to the hills
and let the dying world, die.

We'll walk together
along river banks, through fields,
grow fat and old and drunken
and recall the night the
burning city kept us weary.

Among the Ruins

Among the ruins
of the city, once great,
we forage for food.
Through and under the monuments
of grave dust kings
and long forgotten gods
we stumble upon
a place to lie in wait.

God

Right now God
is failing but you
smell so nice and
the world outside my
door is cold winter
you are warm I have
no light and am
glad to touch your
cheek and breathe.

Moonlight Dreams

tell me what the moonlight dreams
what it cares for
and who it longs to embrace
I see now its shimmering
liquid reflection
does the moon think
and does the wind breathe
a plaintive sigh?

will you sing me
the songs the
coupled angels sing
I will bring you
dandelions and clovers
and a bird with a broken wing

let the sea dry up
let the forests burn

Cranberry Tea

And the sky is tinted like cranberry tea,
you flow like the swift river.
The scent of musk breaks the room
and Homer forgets his simile.

In the Bath-During War

I sit in this tub
filled with warm water
listening to the noises my body makes
and wonder if I'm arrogant
to want you to touch me
to want you to want to
and I wonder if it's vanity
that enrages me
when a male voice answers your phone
although you live alone.
I assure you I am not
the cotton mouthed idiot
who speaks just now
you flip my words
and weave them through your bra-straps
the bumps on the back of
your neck blind me
is it me, or is it the cold?

O golden possibility
I embrace you now
in lieu of flesh and pigment
I take you now
what sprouts just now
the stench of collapse
or the firming of resolve?

War erupts like a blister
across the hobbling globe
can I be no firmer than that
the mere bubbling of passions?
I am firmer than steel that does not break
that cracks the bones of empires
the marrow leaks-it is gobbled up.

PC Room

she looks the same
as everyone else
but that sameness fits
her better than
everyone else
she's a child
eyes closed and mouth open
drips from icicles
expectant and perfect.

Dark Skin

dark skin,
brown and roasted
like almonds
the sugared kind
a voice delicate
and quite airy
gets lost in the wind
while leaves, trampled leaves
roll and tumble off
into oblivion. She grabs
my jacket and tugs.

Sunflowers

there is a girl in Budapest
who says I am like a sunflower
tilting my head at
every sun I happen upon
I don't know if that's true
but it seems odd here
in the painter's room
with snow melting on the bay windows
the tall creaking trees
as slender as her fingers
and the aroma of productivity
tucked away into every corner
yes, I leave bits of my life
scattered across several continents
and my career is as stagnant
as a rank pond in August
but now I listen to the wind
mumbling the sad dirge of eternity
and I will wander where ever
that wind, that voice, eternity take me.

Pigeons

pigeons hop upwards a wind with snowflakes wraps them up
like a warm embrace.
I remember the smell of the Thames dirty, muddy, brown
and you in front of the Tower Bridge your beauty like a warm
and open hand.

The Economy of Ice-cream

The first eager days in Budapest
you led me by the hand
me with virgin eyes
letting the city fill me
with the Danube
crazy Kenny, the Indian boss
and the mumble of street cars
we met the short Eszter
and walked to the ice-cream store
and you went in and treated us
the lady corrected my English
and you laughed. I said
strawberry and the lady-
raspberry. In the
morning, in front of the archives
I asked if you remember
how it was before-before what?
-You know when there was Communism-
-when I was little
you could buy a scoop
for 5 forints and gorge on ice cream.
Now it's 100 forints- you say
and wave your hand, not for the
rising cost, but for the
little girl, chocolate dribbling
down her chin. And today
we sat on the roof of the largest
mall in Hungary, and ate ice-cream
giggling, laughing and I could just
barely make out the little girl

hands stuffed with forints.

Fuck You

fuck you
fucking with my happiness
I don't get off on apathetic jealousy
learn to swim yourself.

A Ja Nie

you don't see me
you look right past me
I want to tear
the image you have of me.

I want to place
my hand in the small
of your back.

but here in my stagnate room
I sit with my impotence.
I curse you, your camel hair jacket
and I curse the
life that scars to death.

Crestfallen

our dreams are crestfallen
half a bottle of wine
shoves clarity in your face
as if the lesson
we learned would ever stick.
I fucked the dregs
of insolvent time
I fucked the dregs
of idealism.

Autoportret

about six feet in stature
but I stoop so really
it's only about 5 ft 8
my hair currently
is not sticking up at odd angles
which it usually does
it is very short
and impossible to tell
from this angle that I'm balding
as for the colour it is a dull brown
the lightness of the summer departing
as I spend more time indoors
dark blue eyes the colour
of an angry sky in July
a strange small nose
which has been variously described
as English whatever that means
or bird-like, more apropos
a mouth which is a little small
but not obviously so
ears which are largish, but in proportion
after a day of not shaving
a healthy growth of stubble
a few freckles which may be overlooked
by the less discerning
and I'm wearing a beige t-shirt

that contains a dog
which is forever breaking the injunctions
not to eat, smoke or be a dog
dark blue jeans, silver watch
and black socks.

In a Canoe

wondering which way to cast
the uncertain prow
of the canoe that glides
effortless beneath me

near the granite rocks
the shallow pools
full of minnows
and crayfish

or to let it drift
to the centre where
there is nothing
but the swiftness
of the river
the gnashing
roaring mouths
of the river

I am a leaf
beneath this foam
I have nothing to offer
you but the uncertainty
of this prow.

A Sigh

a half-forgotten sigh
that I clench in my calloused hand
and it burns and scalds
and knows no relent
all you I owe
and every finger of my hand
is debt.
But is there no happiness?
No whoops of joy?
I beauty the trees
the body abstract
no nothing
not beneath my body now.

A Bruised Apple

a bruised apple sits
in the place where a woman's head should be
the blankets have been torn from the bed
as if in preparation for a ceremony.
but no one ever comes into the room
could I bear the comfort of a solitude destroying creature?
I want a drink
I want a gash
I want to flick off this soul
of a young boy, trembling
scared of the snarling dog

18

when I was 18
I thought I had mastered
the dull plod of years
as they lay-slopping away
just ahead of me
and now as my
hair falls or grays
there is no mastery
over the plodding years
no bridle, no harness
no way to tame them.

Sometimes

sometimes
you ask yourself
why am I here
at this intersection
of lines on a map
and you stir
the dirt with your toes
and look to the left
just over your shoulder
at another horizon-again-
too self aware to wait on
or to expect a response.

Gypsy Man

another late night in Korea
gypsy man restrain
your wandering feet
that dart from one lily pad
to the next. Tie
your wagging tongue to
the fence like the
dog of your youth
that ran off and was
crushed by a semi.
Black fur-red blood
seeping into the pavement.
There is nothing new here-
no flower that slowly blossoms
and charts the progress
of the sun across the sky.

Nunca Sabia

I could say that
I'm happy
and wish on candy floss clouds
that sunlight would be mixed
at a ratio of 2:1:1
with contentment and inspiration.

new vistas open up
beneath me
like the earth has
melted away
and each new mode
as terrifying as the last.
To go. To stay.
To tear up little bits
of me and throw
them to the wind.

My money's on China
and the cold Gobi desert
of Inner Mongolia-
there, maybe under a wind worn rock
a traveler, years hence
will recover the yellowed
parchment of my thigh
and barely make out the words
-nunca sabia-

Memory

every memory
is a snare
a barked hook
an invitation
to resume dining
in the buried halls
of Pompeii
every thought
of that face
of that place
plunges me back
to that familiar
situation
trout out of the water
furious gills
sometimes I wonder
if Rome, Highgate, and Bridgenorth
have collapsed because
I'm no longer there
to hold the strings taut.

So Many Plans

I have so many plans
that I have careful
adequately carved into
the diligent lines of my hands
so many hopes for future satisfaction
mortgaged and deferred
these houses of cards
that'll tumble and collapse
with the slightest change of wind
or with the inevitable tap
of a bony finger
on the unprepared shoulder.

Quite Alone

I am quite alone
in this far realm
the place of my exile
a pilgrim making no
progress, I should progress
to where the sun whips the naked branches
the heartless January winds
but I am bound by contracts
and dotted lines.

The future is a dimly lit room
vague dark shapes loom
and threaten like pregnant clouds.
I wander in the labyrinth
and hope only that the
floor continues to rise
up under each step.

I am a flower dried
between the pages
a living moth, fluttering
pinned to the Bristol board
labelled and categorized.

meanwhile
the primary winds go off
over there, dusting off
the musty smell
of ordinary life.

Blaze

see how I blaze
with white light
and fragments of dust
and grime disappear
I notice my spirit
unfettered-still
as free as any
singing bird.

The Belt

the last cigar burns
held in the crayon coloured hand
the smoke has clouded everything
a man with a paunch is reading
the paper

staring at a dirty wash bin
a reflection contorting the water
a woman with dirt beneath her fingernails
is doing the dishes

there's a belt
thick leather
hanging
just beside the door

what does it threaten?
what does it cajole?

the belt
hung at my uncle's house

Last Night

Last night
in the ever glistening quiet
of the half-forgotten stars
I listened to the night.
Nothing. Then the shudder
of the clouds that scamper across
the eyelid of the moon.
the human Instant
dissolved into the liquid Eternity.

Half caught between youth
and the stream of age
already memory floods up
things once common
have become myth.
I age, and half the mortal
world ages with me.

Lament of the Mourning Dove

How I miss the morning dove
mourner of the shank of evening
of the fat flesh of twilight
would you mourn for me here?
Far from the stoic cliffs of clay
crumbling off into forgetfulness
and the neurotic augury of the waves-
the Lake of Sorrows
where even the birds lament
time seeping off into nothingness.
But sadness here is a farce
accompanied only by the
bitter squawks of pigeons
who have never seen
the skies darken at noon
while the ground is shred asunder
by the gaping box of Hell.
Nor have they ever
pierced their breasts
to slake the thirst of their
pipping brood; and so
can never moan your aria
and let it float up to the open legs of Heaven.
Let me float up with your song
let me see the compassionate God, bending prone,
let me shield my eyes, think of home
if only through the echo of your grief.

Midnight

midnight-
the love throbs of the crickets
a faint half-rain
lying
on a bed
with blankets
and thoughts.

I have been tramping

I have been tramping
past the broken carcass shops
past the outburst of light
the riot of sound and dissonance

I have been tramping
through the liberties
the glowing haze
the gentle buzz
the quiet still

and now I return
to my wounded parapet
that overlooks the city
which chills in the freeze
of mid-afternoon
now see the bustle of
the driven ants
the honks and screeches
of the heady traffic

Walk

I walk these streets
sidewalkless, jammed with cars
everyday, and everyday
I point my body
in the same direction
and legs and arms
fall into line.

I am waiting
for something to happen
applause to erupt
for the city to collapse
and to stumble across myself
somewhere between the yellow leaves
and the stench of the sewer.

Epitaph

My hand pokes up from the grave
or reassembles itself from the ash
and greets you. Lovers of the insoluble.

Down in the Basement

Down in the basement
watching tv we were kissing
which meant something at the time
then her hands darted
along my jeans
and mine along hers

and on it went-
and she brought me a towel
I went down on her
and she went down on me
her clitoris hardening like a ripe fist
then I put my penis between her legs
and made her moan
she's pregnant now, not by me
I don't write this to condemn
or to stir up old desire
but to say that you opened like
the petals of a flower
and only now do I see
the beauty of the opening.

Poem of Seduction

I need players for my drama
I need women to covet
there will come a time
when the vine will wither.
Are you so old as to have touched
every part of me that is a man?
Am I so young that I do not yearn
to be placed in the palm of your hand?
No matter the promises made in haste
before your scent before your taste
be it plague, be it death
the caul thrown off, enthralled,
the arching back, the quickened breath
you I take, take you all
wrap me in your body's shawl.

You Tell Me

you tell me
my touch is like snow
lost in the blizzard of your body
your hands move like spiders
across the web of my body.

My body mourns your absence
while my chest misses
the exploration of your thigh.

you rip
like the sun rips the moon
like the mountains tear the sky.

Dusk My Eyes

dusk my eyes, make my lips as
two safe and warm coves
of the sea, that sea that
stretches infinite
between the two
of us.

dusk my eyes, harbour my regatta
my tall yachts and vivid purple skies
bring them close to your bosom
your breasts that
heave up and down
with the tide of your breath.

I am willingly vanquished, famished, relinquished
a whisper breeds the scuttling of my armada.
Ravish me treacherous rocks of happiness.

Capsize my freighters and destroyers,
wreck their hulls, twist them with your spine
your ways of loving and losing
till I fall down on my knees
and place my lips on the lips
of your sex.

I Remember

I remember you as a whore
your pear shaped breasts
swaying as I fucked you from behind.
You said, use my body
anyway you want to (I didn't).
No one has ever given themselves
so freely, so completely, to me.
Before or since.
I remember the huge raindrops
falling on the leaves of
the maple in the drive. Thud. Thud.
I remember my penis between your breasts-
and you licking. Two strangers,
imprinted in my mind-outtakes
from a ridiculous porn film.
I remember you standing at the end of the drive
a single tear running down your cheek
thinking I would see those breasts again,
the mole on the curve of your neck
that I mistook for a piece of lint.

Just Because

just because I like you
doesn't mean I want to fuck
and just because I want to fuck
it doesn't mean
I am another in
the long line of men
who came as soon as you blinked
just because you're beautiful
your smile a happy tug
doesn't mean that
there are no possibilities
dark ladies in dim corners
unmet futures that
I could still yet choose
and just because
my comfortable shoes
and unkept hair are
no indications of my character
doesn't mean that I
don't dress up well
and just because my life
doesn't go from a to b to c
doesn't mean I'm irresponsible.

Contagious

contagious breath
unreal breasts
I can almost
taste the touch
of your skin
on my palm.

The Caravaner's Dream

Here lies the waste
here lay the drought lands
my water has gone
there's nothing left to rub
across my chapped lips.
How am I to trek across
the frightening wilderness alone?
Without the honey I licked from my fingers
it seems like decades ago?
I know I will survive the attempt
skeletal, vulture scarred
and drag myself over the line
that parts the brown of the desert
from the green of the oasis.
But where is the camel
I seem to have known since childhood.
I won't go without the dancing girl
who looked up with her eyes
which scalded in their intensity
who took the silver piece
I rubbed across her palm and smiled.
I will not go, to be blinded by the sun,
to die a dog's death.
Find another bastard for your caravan.
Love has made me lazy.
Not just love, but the memory of it.

Sometimes I close my eyes
and can see her lying under me
eyes closed and face reddening
and she speaks in a language
which is neither mine nor hers
but somewhere in the middle
and her legs tighten around me-
but up from these dreams.

Resurrection

The big dipper skirts
the star infested sky
while night pounces soft on
an abandoned garden-drought bitten
with cracked tile earth-dry season leprosy.
A few mere pilgrims wandered
through the expanse of the desert
and saw their tracks disappear
behind them, covered up in red sand
or covered up with dry snow.
Quick entry to the desolation
and just as quick abandonment.
Beneath the sand, beneath the snow
an ancient empire lurks, it cracked
and collapsed ages since, its language
long reduced to the babble of a dried up creek
its bones mingle with the dust and sleet.

But then some Merlin's daughter
or sister or mother or teacher of everything
passes through these parts, clouds
sudden swirl, and a quick rain
violent departs from the sky and pounds
the fragile earth, that laps up the water
like a drowning man. And the stalks
of withered oaks and maples wake up

as if out of some arboreal nightmare
while the strong roots flow up
between the cracks of the cobbles
and the trees flash quick green
the leaves blazing like flames.
You come into this room, this garden, my body
with tiny, well formed ears
upturned breasts like cat eyes
soft gold hair above the lips
where smiles break like waves
crash, explode up against the rocks.
And my body, once ruined
begins to turn back to spring
to resurrect-

To Ola, Gone

It's night. Not too late. Not too early. I sink. Sink into that familiar state that no power can allay that no power can shake off. I have called it depression before and conjured up the dog with mange not black-more an off brown. I have said it stalks me that I've suffered immensely-oh-oh-I've said these things and will probably put them forward again but all this reeks to me of choice. I would like your pity-soft like the brush of your hand across my cheek especially when I look up at you with puppy dog eyes rimmed with wetness. Tears in which only I have faith but you greet me with the hard rebuff of your happiness which is neither cruel nor callous but which lacks the pregnant tenderness of one putting on a show of loving and oh how fond I am of shows. This morning, Ola, I happened upon a nervous butterfly. It was flapping wildly about our bedroom. I don't know where it came from all of the windows were closed. Anyway, it was just me and this butterfly and I helped him, her, it to escape. The giant hands of the liberator bringing no consolation to this creature desperately trying to smash itself against the false sky. I thought about us and how we feel about each other about the word love which is thrown about in this here world like it were an indefinite article about how it is a beautiful, yet somewhat nervous butterfly which people, in their unthinking goodness try to pin down, still live, wings flapping to the clinical severity of the Bristol board. So live with me-move in with me here and let us many pleasures prove especially those which are the most iffy and conductive to productive research. We'll let the butterflies tumble about clearly undefined, but still healthy for all that. I know I ask you this from vanity, selfishness plus the desire to fill up these nights when solitude confronts me with a hard statue stare but couldn't it be marvelous despite all that? Because many good things are achieved through atrocious motives and our bed-the one that provides a chorus when we fuck has a lineage that stretches back-way back. Carted back from Warsaw by a man hitch-hiking and it passed from generation to generation of felicitous fuckers of which we are but the most recent though odds are good we won't be the last. Does this ancient artifact alone entice you? To tumble into my arms? Into my rooms? If not that then the dent you'll put in this solitude. If not that then these poems I place between the silence of your sigh and the emptiness of your thigh but mostly to slay that impious red clanging beast that causes you to tremble and sway so. And so easily will I become St. George my lovely princess of the dirty feet for thee so climb up just behind and ride the dragon with me, and we'll roar off in the dusty dregs of eternity.

She Says

She says she's naked under her clothes
she points to another girl's breasts
and asks what I think about those.

Three Apocalypses

1
the great beast laughs-lunges
furiously whips its tail
spews out its entrails
the stars drop like rain
the laughable geometry of angles
right, obtuse, slight
and everything is gathered up again
like a hand cupping grain
and spewed out into the vast empty
the interstellar vomit
is stuck to the blank of the deep
and all is formed again
only awaiting the next passage
through the serpentine intestines
of the beast

2
death smells like a woman
string of pearls around her neck
and rose petals in her cunt
death dribbles-saliva
dangling at the corners
of the mouth-a lecherous
old man with white
hair and black pubes
touching his limp dick
the damp rotten smell of sex
dangling in the breeze
like a guillotine blade

death is the nervous cumshot
into the eager hand.

3
my body is a lake
a party but all the guests
are sullen
streamers and pieces of soggy cake
float in the shallows.

my body is an invitation
but none have r.v.s.p'd
and I sit in numerous closets
forgotten, unwanted and gathering dust.

my body is an 'if only I had'
conditional-hypothetical
and all of my potentialities
are pieces of hair
from my balding head
curling up into dust bunnies.

o dust
o drought
o dry season.

The savannah is thirsty.

A Strange Air

my bedroom has a strange air
it breeds strange dreams
of lions and mauled villagers
and inept local cops.

It breeds strange dreams
obese black women trapeze
and inept local cops
sex in public, like the bums in Lodz

Obese black women trapeze
I wake up with dirty sheets
sex in public, like the bums in Lodz
I call her big bertha and her belly jiggles.

I wake up with dirty sheets
my bedroom has a strange air
I call her big bertha and her belly jiggles
of lions and mauled villagers.

Bill and Ailene

Dear Ailene
lazy and fat
take out the trash.

I will not remove
all of your empties
you welfare bum
do it yourself.

I may drink
this is true
but is only to spare myself
the wicked sight of you.

as if a man
who looks like cat vomit
flattened by a train
can be choosey where he lies.

damn fine looking vomit
I am. Just last night
a colleen came up to me
and murmured in
a voice fraught with lust
'what a man!' 'what a man!'

either she was stunned
by how God could be so cruel to the world
or she was a pro with a quota to fill
did she, perchance leave a bill?

at last we touch upon a theme
of which you may have some knowledge
how to make men cream
on a nightly basis for fun and for profit.

oh bill

oh ailene

this can only end

in divorce

and I have neither the money

nor the will

so let it end

again

between the sheets

so I can finish in a minute

and I can get some sleep.

Refusal

I refuse to live my life
between the lines
It won't do me no good
like drinkin' terpetine.
There's a man in a telfon suit
counting coins
there's a drunken monster
errupting from my loins.

Wash my face in the river Lethe
tear the world asunder with my teeth
Cast away the thoughts clanking
around in your hollow head
and lie with me baby on your
cast iron bed.

I hear the tales trippin'
from your tepid tongue
that you use to beat the dark with
but your trembling voice
makes me wanna come
your the rind, I'm the pith.

You Linger

you linger beneath my eyelids
you tarnish my purest thoughts
you ravish me without relent
I would destroy the moon
smother the fire of the sun
pluck out the many eyes of Heaven
descend into Hell and smite the dog dragon multitude
all these hallucinations-
the small mounds of flesh
pink nipples rise up.

Sonnet to my dick

this blue veined
useless thing
lies limp
I doubt its efficacy
in amorous affairs
but it does its duty
stands at attention
when aroused
gives idle pleasure
on rainy days
I am alone
even with my dick, my cock, my penis, my wee-wee, etc.
when we were young
of course young and stupid
our penis' were marks of pride and envy
yours is big
mine is small
then came puberty
dreams of perfect romance
my god I wanted you
your beautiful lips
and soul
I betcha you
never heard that before
eating Kentucky Fried Chicken
being chased by bees
and my cock hanging limply
throughout.

Her Neck

her neck is pale
and a black string is tied
around it
I am looking at a leaf
trapped in her sweater
when I see them
as she turns
two plump breasts
and the crucifix that
dangles between them

How Love Starts

this is how love starts
you notice the nervous twitch
of her cheek
the flicker of her smile
you gave at the same flame smouldering
you kiss
you melt into one another.

then you notice
how her breasts cup in your hands
her slender fingers
weave themselves along your spine.

and love grows pound by pound
until it is a weight you almost can not bear
her legs smooth and endless
her ass smooth and firm
your fingers along her opening
she moans quietly.

and she lets you stagger awhile
with the weight of your love
lets you pretend she shares the same burden
and she picks up the toys involved in the game
and her pretension trails off
but whatever you bear for her keeps on throbbing
like the pain of an amputated arm.

that is how love stalls

Kasia

Kasia, with your head turned down-
you look like liquid ocean-
you look like sunshell sea-
please turn over-
I have something I would like to show you.

Your Bed

last night we laid in your bed
with the fog dissolving clarity
today we left for the airport
a baby was being sung to
we talked about useless things

now I remember you dancing
your tears falling like broken spines
last night we laid in this bed.

Slender Fingers

long slender fingers
razor wire smile
gone now
like a ghost
or a too friendly dream.

Old Crocodiles

The crunching steps
the first sticking snow
the one that will last past
December and into January
a woman and a man
walk through the white
walk past the brown
relics of summer's profusion
look straight up
the somersaulting snow
as hypnotic as any
siren's song.
The stories these two
could tell- between
the lines of arrival
and departure
of lives lived, imagined
and defeated.
These two souls
much the same
like two old
crocodiles who float
familiar next to each other
with hardly a hand raised
or stutter of difference.

Sit

Sit with me and say nothing
I prefer your silence to the empty chatter of horse faced women
and manure stained ideas.

Come down with me to the gap, that Hades that terrifies,
the gap where nothing can be expressed but silence.

Knowing You

knowing you
as I do
thinking in the other room
intent
awake.

For Hilary

I don't like poems, she shrugs.
Troublesome, yeah, but I agree.
Poetry nullifies erections.
It is a thing for frigid church matrons
who host functions and strawberry socials.
It is a stillborn spring
sumac bit with blight.
My mistress you have cast me out,
the last member of my withered tribe.

Paint and Bra Straps

I tear the paint from the door
like I want to tear the bra
from your shoulder.
I realize this is infinite folly
and yet I persist
like an old man, who,
confronted with the truth of his truth
confidently twiddles his thumbs
making you suspect
his truth isn't what you thought it to be.

To Hilary, Departing

I have no wealth or fame
to compel you to me
nor no gaudy plumage
to lure you to me

I am a ragged
unwashed troubadour strumming
timidly under your window.

I can only give you
my essence
the substance of my being
the parent of these words.

In a hundred years after
we have slipped the bounds
of mortal flesh
and wealth and fame
become common and lie
wide open in the city brothel

all who ever loved you
will be brought before you
they will be revealed
in their honest selves
some dull and withered
some baroque and radiant.

Then I will have
my gaudy peacock feathers
my coins of gold and silver
my chains of amber

and these my humble words
will again fall on your half-closed ears
and my chest will again rise
and bubble with hope.

Forgive Me

listen to the purple wind
that now rages like a carnivore
that now limply flutters like a butterfly
envelop me now with your harsh dissonance
that now trickles slow like sap
that gushes now like the spring torrent
flow me through your liquid brain
let me rummage, pour me through its chasms,
forgive the dreck, recoil the scald of war boiling.

After Naruda

I wanna tell you 'bout how
God made the earth and the moon
how he tore the continents apart
to forge the seas
'bout how he gave me
a flower that unfolds in my hand
that does to me
what spring does to the cherry tree.

Let Me Dance

Let me dance like a whirlwind
on your skin let me trace
with my little finger the paths
of my reckless pilgrimages.

If I happen to grow
like a perfumed cedar
among the cracks of your spine
don't be surprised-
the country is fertile there.

If I should happen to rise
in the middle of your Castilian night
like a misplaced sun-
don't be alarmed
that's just impatience.

Without you in it
this entire country
is a prison cell
and I tick off
the days minutes hours
of my sentence.

but with you I soar and I hover
I fit into freedom like a seagull
with complete liberty.

I need the abundance of your arms
the gentle rain of your kisses
the flooding of your tears.

Blank Page

The blank page seduces me
the subtle fascism of line and period.
My bank account trickles to nothing
and I consider options I've
already fled from. But this
woman keeps me warm and
I don't mind pushing a broom for her.

Night Shift

I work late at night.
A woman sleeps in a bed
waits for me.
As she sleeps
I vacuum, dust,
scrub out toilets.
She dreams of fountains,
landslide kisses.
When I return I brush
against her cheeks,
hold her in my arms
and I try not to wake her.

Furiously

Furiously, she strikes.
The empty cardboard fills
ocean of blue.
I tell her I was a poet once
and wore golden shoes.
She shrugs.

Harbour

A song plunges me
into the warm waters
of your harbour and bounty
I'd like to touch your hand
if only for a moment briefly
between here and the hereafter
two passengers dwindling
melting down into one.

I do nothing all day
but scratch out these poems
with the palpitations of my heart
and they ferment, jettison
and orbit around our barrio

in the cross hairs of lust and fidelity
the barrel pressed against my breast
I beg you mercy o demons of indifference
deliver me from anything but
complacency and indifference.

Your World

This is the world you inhabited
before I knew the boundaries
of your flesh
this how things were
before the discovery.

There was Valladolid
cobbles worn smooth
in the quivering, ancient heart
surrounded by los pajaros
smog choked palpitation.

There was Villanubla
the fuente de los Angeles
the adobe houses
the grandmother threatened
and the dead strung up
on the road to Valladolid
for the crows to feast upon.

There was the mother
and there was the father
the field worker, the truck driver
the cement mixer
there was the brother
office worker, waiter, cook in the army
now with two kids
there was the sister
sometimes sane, the other one
a hair dresser in Madrid
and you

who filled up notebooks
with dairies, stories
and poems
about possessed houses
and Great Auks.

While where the sun sets
I was doing somewhat the same
now I've stepped over the horizon
like Cortes in reverse
while from my window
float gypsy sounds and smells.
I close my eyes,
inhale and listen.

We Three

sinead on the stereo
sings of ireland
pili at the table
reads spanish compositions
I am trying to write a poem
a muscle atrophied and unflexed
lighted windows like open eyes
sinead with guilt reconciles herself
pili with prepositions and subjunctive
me, myself, meanwhile
rummage through the empty, yet
filling corridors.

-Ist

the keys lying
on your desk
harbour no philosophies
but they seem more pregnant
than the silence between us.

Living with You

not quite happy
not quite content
and yet not desperate
living with you
dreaming of someone else

through no lack of love
not on your part nor on mine
just a desire to grab
the dangling carrot
and to sink my teeth
into the apple of my demise

I know I feel something
I trap myself in circles
do I really want what
I can't have, or is it
I trap myself in circles
I know I feel something

living with you
dreaming of someone else.

Sugar Rush

She says on the phone
she's got a sugar rush
but loves me more than ever
and can love be compartmentalized
and restrained?
You should read the poems
I've written, she casually
mentions-they're great.
You've written poems?
I also write poems
about cities, rocks and the sea-
are you jealous of these?

The End

so this is it then-the end
there's nothing left
for us to do but
crumble
like giant, marble pilars
roofless, that say
to the passing centuries
that one once upon a time
somebody thought this
place was special.

I never wanted
it to end
short of death
and maybe not
even then
But I am free now
to follow scents
in the wind.

Your pictures are gone
from the wall
and I notice the
empty spaces.

Soul

I never wanted to own your soul
like it was a piece of meat
or a bit of land wedged
in between the curves of the river.
I only wanted to grow up with you,
to change with you, as the seasons change
but you wanted to go off,
after each new thing
like a puppy chasing its tail.
You made me promise to never leave you
and I never did.
And now I will never believe
the best of words until
I see footsteps falling into line

The First Poem

the first poem is the hardest
the moment before the plunge
the delicious uncertainty
I have never woken up
beside you sleeping
though god I want to
that the aftermath of these moments
I asked the conquesting stars
how they entice the shy planets to dance
a mute and silent response
so dance with me until the timid light fades away
until the forever night swallows up
the tender sighs of the stumbling day.

And Now

and now after the deluge
I take up my pen to describe
the little garden my bed has become
humble, modest and alive
lit by the candles of your eyes
whose blues waters hop out
and spread among the ferns
that your presence has enlivened
and if I am too wild in your praise
too eager for things so soon to fit together
know how long I wandered
in the dimly starred night
biding my time with the creatures of the dark
then your sudden sun
flames up the dull sky, washes it blue
blue the colour of a lake in July
blue the colour of your eyes.

No, I don't think so

No, I don't think so
I don't think I could ever
get tired or bored of you-
not through any great virtue
just that I've wandered countless years
like a faithless Israelite
through these self-created, self-imposed deserts
in constant search of the next change
that will complete me, fulfill me.
Now I realize the idleness of those changes
of those beaten down paths through the grass
that intersect like lace through the
confines of this old and dusty heart.
So here I stand, firm like Luther
in the forest of my insecurities
firm to shirk them off and grasp at happiness
firm to try the faithful vessel
firmly praying, firmly hoping
the timid boat always nudges
just up against your gentle shore.

I Cut an Island

I cut an island.
My tailor s shears
sharp, diligent
plunged along the line
of sea and cliff.
I spiced this isle
with mangroves
and the trickle of streams.
None dared trespass.
A silver heron
the neck elegant, slender
wings like an embrace
alighted. It chose this isthmus.
It chose me. The flutter
of the wings completes my labour,
completes me.

Two Bergs

two bergs
float on the midnight sea
dark as any dream
migrant birds
snatch a few moments of rest
the saline saturated air
cleansing their lungs
and perhaps those two bergs
rub up against each other
the frozen desire of hydrogen + oxygen
and what is tender for them
is an icequake for the startled birds
who jet up to the dull, night foggy sky
and set off, again, to find some other shelter.
But which are we? The moulting birds
or the burning ice?

Get Up

Get up, you whisper,
sleep in your navy eyes
parked between the dark spark of concern
and the little light one of joy.
Let that one go, the light one,
let it be tinder for forest fires
let it happen upon dry and ripe kindling
like that day deep in the countryside
of what was Kent County
when my dad and me set the rows
of cedars ablaze. He shrugged.
It was a proud shrug.

The Idea of a Smile

There's the idea of a smile
lurking behind your lips.
Maybe it waits for the spring
the April torrents
strong currents
gulped up by the dirt
to poke its green spear
up to the light.
Or maybe it's waiting
for my hand on your hip
and a dip into your eyes
Cool like a breeze
off a field covered with snow.

My Descent Into Madness

I shall describe for you
my descent into madness.
I shall mark all points
of consequence with a star*.
Omitting only those parts
which offend more puritanical ears.
I shall render in
great detail the full extent
of my moral, physical
emotional and spiritual decline.
The story shall be told
(appropriately enough) as a
travelogue through time,
explaining; again in great detail
the numerous vices caused
by the illness.
But you of course being
the ever-friendly reader will hear
a full account of it all.

A Jest

I have placed
my happiness on this
wooden throne
splinters and slivers
pray do not break under the weight
and what luscious joy
can I suck from thee?
My happiness placed like a crown
burdened brow
don't stumble like a twitching drunk
I love thee-I desire thee-
I need thee and thine
pale chalk outline completes me
Do not abandon me to the
wilderness of self, solitary
let's go down together
arm entwined in arm
in the velvet and well-appointed casket.

The Silent Hunter

Beware of the silent hunter
that comes alone in the night
like a stranger in a bar
that stalks with the stubborn paint of words
and rings the stale, maybe broken bells
of your desire of your lust.
He'll take your empty life, maybe your wretched heart.
You decide which is more problematic.
He'll fill them with
phantasms of light
creatures of the dawn.
I have no comfort for you.
He's coming. He'll get you.

On Ingesting a Continent, Whole

The pictures are melting off the walls
and fall in to their own severed rhythm
my head hurts and I rub my sore eyes.
Nothing here is real-
not the belching chasms growing in my floor
not the torso of a woman
floating just above my head.

The mundane nightmare
the un-terrified loop of a dragon swerving
I in numbness
I have seen everything in threesome harmony
the hell is in this, and nothing else.

But then all that is shattered
and thrust into some new and horrible heaven
Hussars erupt, screech,
their horses trod you, and crush your skull
a yellow badge, a star of David
pinned to your lapel
and you thinning, withering
into a thing half-human.

peace.
joy.
god loves us all.

Not as a Mother

Not as a mother
more as a jaded nightwalker
who stays out all night
playing poker-truck stops
"they've surrounded us boys"
more as a guffaw than
a call to arms
paradisio eyes
smile like a crowded breeze
she could get away with murder
and she has
late princess of Muncey First Nation
lately of church street at Maple Leaf
Gardens.

Yellow

I would clothe you in yellow
yellow like the warm solar embrace
and fish for you in closets
and rummage sales,
if you would return to me
the interest on the capital
and flee with me to the places where the light is dim
places plagued by mildew cobwebs
and the shivering, trembling hand
barking creatures erupting
sprouting from our chests
but the truth is, I have
nothing to offer you except these
dusty dreams and the skins
I routinely shed.

Before

Before the beginnings
before the endings
and after them both
beyond, below and above time
the wholeness rests
and shudders violently
in this paradox:
two babies are born
the Creator and the Destroyer
the Creator says: behold
I make the clouds of dust
and the Destroyer replies
I am where the dust is not.
The Creator boasts
I will defeat you with stars-
I am the death of stars-
and planets, I make planets-
I am the death of planets-
see the stirrings, that's life-
-and I am its end.

I saw the sun descend

I saw the sun descend
the painted bird wither
and I wept.

I saw a black snake
and a white snake
wrestle or make love
in a round pond
and I was amazed.

I heard the rain drops
beat like the throb of the earth drum
and you took me in
and made me a little less cold.

And in that make shift shelter of bones
and bark I came upon myself
as if in a cracked mirror.
I was still so far from home-
like a drowning fish.

Immune

I don't wanna feel immune
like a fly in a glass of spit
I don't wanna be a hypocrite
I wanna believe in dreams
like Queen Mab, fairy queen
hear your faint little scream.
I want an adventure
I want you
I want you.

Waltz

truth can be
constructed like paper mache
truth can be constructed
it's a waltz-two steps
forward-one back.
truth is scary
scary scare crow eyes
and only one bird
one venturesome bird
guesses the lie.

No Damnation

A man with no hope for
damnation, turns
as he enters this
machine.

Twists tightly
opens his palms and
dunks, devastates.

Looks to the east, again
enters into family compacts
views through the finder
eats what is offered
roams through the lands
twists yet again
on the planks
narrowed and splintered.

Lunch Break

lunch break
a bug from Asia
crawls from back to front
a bug from Asia
she looks, sour
c'mon it's easy
her head, heavy
smile to frown
a bug from Asia

On Getting a Hair Cut

Our hero enters her den
eager, like a hog bursting a pen
expecting nothing more mundane
expecting nothing in his brain
than a simple little trim
that a bright chimp could have given him.
But fate chooses the days she will
and more awkwardly-she has chosen this
for the innocent-for the unsuspecting
for the tarantula's foul kiss!
That Gorgon with badly applied make-up
That Gorgon with hair dye still drying
in the hairs of her malicious head.
The one with the quailing, flabby arms
this is the one, on valiant hero
that you have to vanquish, to confront.
She flies at him with Polish,
he parries with hesitant English
that he would like if at all possible
and convenient, both practically
and in regards to star signs
to get his hair cut. 'Rozumiem'.
That dragon speaks, with belch of fire
or belch of garlic and perogie smoke.
She sits him down, up he tries to rise
but she thrusts him back down

now with firm, rock steady grasp.
She has you in her clutches
like an innocent, bleating lamb
and like the same you will be shorn.
She's deaf to your hesitation, reserve
but most of all to your complaint.
She wields her scissors as if
she were a drunken samurai reject
and her aim is just as good
now perilously close to the ear
now again perilously close to the ear
and now again a third time perilously close to the ear.
'Damn it woman!' Our hero exclaims.
'Bardzo dobrze, no?' the bitch replies
'o yes, it's nice it's grand
to slice off one ear, I understand
it's the finest fashion in the land
but for myself, being from foreign climes
I prefer the pair of them.'
And every minute stretches off
into the region of hours
but still her powers never fail
still her arms never cease to flail.
Courage, noble abandoned hero
let loose the quiet, concerned cough.
That deformed statue laughs. Razor whacking
she slices through the skin, she slices
like boiling water poured through winter ices.

Madam, our angered hero must depart
vengeance burning through his burning heart.

Twelve Things to Buy with My Last Twenty Bucks

A boomerang so I can commit suicide creatively.
Cheap alcohol so I don't care or know I'm broke.
A Halloween mask so no one catches on
that the smelly, bloody pulp is me.
A copy of Remembrances of Things Past
(see point number two).
A used magic eight ball to get myself out of this mess.
A very small, undemanding dog. For company.
An atlas, full of places I'm not going to.
A sprig of hemlock, but with my luck,
I suppose it's out of season.
A ticket for an exhibition of sharp, and deadly weapons.
A discounted blow job from a syphilitic whore.
A spoon, because you never know
when someone is going to offer soup.
A pencil, to write a newer, better me.

Things to do in the Mall

Tell them it's all a lie.
No one can put happiness in a bottle
that you can spray on your shoulder.
And you can sharpen your keys all you want
the woman with the come hither look
is never going to ask you to come thither.
Sit on a bench, beside the umbrella plants
take off your clothes, pretend to ferociousness,
spit at the security.
(Make them feel they are earning their minimum wage).
Pinch the screaming infants and toddlers
(give them something to really holler about).
Avoid eye contact with people you met one once upon a time
five minutes. Drunk. At a party. Can't remember your name.
Slice a knife across your palm.
Flick the blood at passerbys.
Give them something real. Something not a lie.

Things Not to Say

I'm dumping you because
you smell like an abattoir
or a field freshly sprayed with pig manure.
I'm dumping you because
your idea of a good time is depilation
followed by a vinegar afterwash.
I'm dumping you because
two wrongs don't make a right.
(but three do) I'm dumping you
(and stealing your plasma television) because
theft is the severest form of flattery.
I'm dumping you because
you have a face fit for internet radio.
I'm dumping you because
you once confessed to homicidal tendencies.
I'm dumping you because
I'm a jack in your three card deck
a pawn on your eight square chess board.

Reasons Not to Bathe

Because the ripe stench
would go in and out like the waves of the tide.
Because my armpits would be like the rainforests
the life-giving mists raise and fall
on the grateful ecosystems of height and levels.
Across the bare desert of my back
would progress dust mites and happy infestations.
I would glory in my odour-like a handshake
or a firm and friendly slap on the back.
People would stand beside me, shamed and say nothing.
My fragrance would surround me, go before me-
I like a universe, I containing untold millions, thousands.
With the money I collect,
having been liberated from the tyranny
of lighter than air bubbles, lilac bathing salts
I could donate to earnest campaigns to eradicate uncleanliness.
Then I could shed clothes, telephone bills,
obligation and burden
and unchain my primal self. My rage of stench
would be another stage in the evolution of man
from frightened ape into fearless stink cloud.
I would be an angler-fish man.
Food and good things would flow into my maw.
In sum-Homo Tempus Novus.

With no Electricity

You can burn stupid books
and warm your hands by the fire.
You can run into the arms
of someone you barely know
and use it as an excuse.
You can listen to the stars
as they dazzle above your head.
You can be a real man
and massacre things in the dark.
Rub your hands together,
feel the warmth.
Sob. (No one will know it's you).
Search for a candle,
and stub your toe.
Think of all the things
you could have said/might have said
and say them.
Invent a new form of Braille
Nipples-commas. Thighs-full stop.
Listen to the sounds in the dark.
Interrogate them.
Design billboards for the blind.
Escape.

A Macabre Alphabet

A is for arsenic slipped unnoticed into soup.

B is for ball-point pens stabbed into throats.

C is for c-4 blowing someone to smithereens.

D is for dynamite doing the same.

E is elevator cords snapped and plunging.

F is for football fan drunk and on the prowl.

G is for guitar string garrottes.

H is for hockey sticks stuffed in dark places.

I is for icicle stabbed into the chest.

J is for Jesus judgementally judging a rope bridge.

K is for killer practising his swing.

L is for lion licking his lips.

M is for monster, genetically altered and mutated.

N is for nostrils filled up with liquid nicotine.

O is for orgasm on a sewing machine.

P is for pencil, protruding from the pancreas.

Q is for kumquat- rancid and obscene.

R is for robot ravaging the land.

S is for a sniper's desperate last stand.

T is for tiger-they're great!

U is for underwear hung for the gate.

V is for volcano-paradise by the sea.

W is for weathervane-gangrene in the knee.

X is for x-rays aimed at the heart.

Y is for yoke smothering you dead.

Z is for deranged zookeeper giving crocodiles something to chew.

A Vincent Price Sonata

In the time of robots
giant killer spiders
will stalk us
our bodies will provide
shelter and nourishment
for arachnid larvae.
Pale impressionable vampires
will feast upon our necks
and deranged wolf men
will howl at helium balloons
floating in the sky, reflecting silver light
and obese alien offspring
will watch all this on their flat screens.

Magpie

magpie
white and black
find my love
bring her back

is she in the birch tree
tall and white?
that shakes in the wind
that bends in the night?

or she's in the wind
that shakes the corn
dead on the stalks
that poke up through the snow.

magpie
white and black
find my love
bring her back.

Prospero Speaks

I left you with cat tails
and crocuses
woven through your hair
like some feral child.

You had a mud splattered face
and a diet of
orange rinds and finger nail clippings.

What is the profit of a curse?
Of banishment from civil and severe
society?

Garter snakes, muskoka rattlers
wetlands, drylands
the delusions of taste
the sting of curry
the bark of cinnamon

I threw you down three flights
head bouncing, indelicate eggshell
a dull, buoyant thud.

"Say anything but that."

Out into the slate dark
fled like a stillborn
hugging the stripped frozen hills

punishment afflicts the exile
like gonorrhoea or the clap
(it nourishes the sadist)

no, I can not forgive you
it is not in my nature to forgive
it is my nature to punish
and yours to be punished.

Where is the shame in the lion's claws
the pity in his razored teeth?

What the Drunk Man Said

I couldn't think
of an epithet
so I called it love.

Disorder

I want disorder to be served with tea
I want to hear your fading plea
I want to wear red socks instead of green
I want the nice old pope to be mean
I want the knives for sacrifice to be clean

I want chaos to flood the streets
I want the oceans to be choked with peat
I want your crooked ace to be beat.

Paris

A found poem

native curious
mediocre pure
romantic beautiful
long favourite
geological different
good rude
English Anglais
pompous ridiculous
bad negative
hardest grateful
snobbish independent-minded
frank deserted
spontaneous proper
urban excellent
better compact
multicultural buzz.

Paris 2

found poem

destination terms
capital places
writer Paris
London years
home Montparnasse
artists Picasso
Modigliani spirit
people cafe
notepad period
attempts establishment
art culture
museum editor
city world
view architecture
streets building
end fact
motorist pedestrian
challenge road
emporium kinds
specimens butterflies
people launderette
clothes machine
number memory
room coins
stuff beggar
lady door
word owner
reason bar

hand ritual
customers hours
food interior designer
beauty stone
vigilance quality
secret tribes.

Paris 3

found poem

is asked
tell means
reveal lived
feel do
went suppose
tend stay
survives must
see scribbling
has attempts
keep say
affected become
was thought
changed find
are finished
enjoy favours
be cross
called sell
buy sums up
put committing
walk feed
could steal
would stop
told greeted
took entered
shaking roaring
gave in began
pre-empt get on
following greet

spend discussing
long make
create discover
like follow
robs.

Paris 4

found poem

still the
so we
those on
with to
us them
their in
and through
although for
or at
than I
what about
it that
even though
since of
own however
rather maybe
something by
not any
because there
over whom
own every
my then
now they

Stardust Suicide

I worked at a job for minimum wage
I lost my leg that set the stage
for me to go on workman's comp
I don't smile much but I've got my health

They sit in their chairs
like they're takin' a bath
a man more a mannequin
is telling me to fast
no stardust primadonna suicide
no stardust primadonna demise

Indefensible

there is nothing
that can be said
in defense of
the wife the kids
the two car garage
the vapid mall.

Deface

a blank page
without the scratchings of ink
is seductive like
a woman in a bathrobe
I have an urge
to deface all such pages
in all such books.

Boring

I'm boring
I'm stale
I've got an old man's tale
I go rooting through the jungle
for a wiff of you
though I find many spices
and fragrant perfumes
of great expense
I'm still no closer to you.

there's Adam
there's Eve
on an old man's sleeve
getting caught in the brambles
those purple thorns
hoping for a peep
of the skin she shed behind.

dudo ergo sum

dudo ergo sum
is a lie
you can tell
'cause it's in latin
father of lies
calm and reposed
your lines, your webs
maybe not webs, but nets
maybe not nets but lines
a line is a line is a line
but the truth is, a truth is
doubt may be honest
but it's easy-faith is hard
and the joke is-Sylvia Path
desperately wanted to laugh.

Vultures

no, vultures are not lesbians
but something more sinister
circling circling
for a sniff of flesh
with no other meaning
than the tip of the wing.

Death

I am not scared of death
whose little green tendrils
no one may escape.
This is what I fear
that I may never kiss
your lips again
yours or remarkably like yours
never taste in love again
be banished to the shadows
where cold women lay waiting
for two or three cold
death denying moments.
I do not deny death
the chilly kiss none may dodge
but I would prefer to have
something to affirm, to laud,
some jarring slap to the face
given with a leer
to the grave, to the tombstone.

Aileen

Aileen stands on the gravel shoulder
of county road number 15
she looks the part, leather mini skirt, red halter top.
A mauve peterbilt pulls up next to her
like a boat floats up to a dock.
A guy with a dusty ball cap rolls down the window.
He waves her over, she steps up.
They get in the back of the cab
empty molson cans, a few packs of players
a cheap blow job he gets a little too rough
Aileen fumbles for her purse, for something in her purse.
The gun, cold, erupts twice, hits him in the stomach.
She searches his wallet, grabs two c-notes
dives into the forest-is gone.

Breech Birth

She said it was because of the breech birth.

It couldn't have been because of Daddy Pedophile
who hung himself in prison after kidnapping
an 8 year old boy and sodomizing him.
It couldn't have been the mother
who ran away after three months.

It couldn't have been the Granddaddy
who beat her with his belt so hard
she would bleed from her buttocks.

It couldn't have been the blowjobs
she was giving to the neighbourhood boys at the age of 9.

It couldn't have been the rape at age 13
and the home for unwed mothers in Detroit.

It couldn't have been the frozen nights
alone, cursing in the broken down Chevy.

This world is evil, she said.
Must have been the breech birth.

Happy Man

The last happy man
in the universe
smiled a crooked grin,
filled his glass with gin
and pulled the trigger.

Lilacs

They say if you clip lilacs
death will come knocking.
I picked some this morning
while I was walking.
Fragrant, purple in bloom.
I'll put them on my table
to lighten the room.

Cracks

looking at the cracks
in the paint
on the ceiling
every one like a wound
inflicted or self-inflicted
every one trailing blood.

Laureate

I tire of our illustrious laureate
his foibles, his renunciation of desire,
whose lies twist round the collective breast.
It is possible to be happy.
Happy even
with the stench of crematoriums
and the rattle of packed cattle cars.

Dark Thoughts

They smell their prey-
these dark, dark thoughts.
They assail me. Go away.
Haven't you gorged enough
on the metallic taste of my marrow?
Drop off now, like fattened fleas.
Fall there, where ever it is that
parasites go to breed.
More real than a hammer shattering glass
this coal black bile-to throw it up and out of me-
to become clean again, pure again
(if I ever was). The shudders stop.
Cold sweaty shivers. Reprieve.
Now again the heaving. The infection lingers.

Lies

there are lies you tell
to yourself
there are lies you tell
to neighbours, friends, third parties.

I am fat I am ugly I am misshapen
I am unlovable I am unwise
I am young and stupid
and old beyond my years.

Really.

I've travelled, I've seen
cotton growing in cotton fields
in Florida and men selling
talking drums, with a ping-ping-ping
on road sides in India.

and so you split yourself
and lose your virginity in Paris
too lazy to climb on top
and you take a picture
of the ceiling you
were looking at
while all of this, all of us,
transgressed.

who are you trying to kid?

Crystalline

early morning
crystalline
clumps of down feather snow
descend
from the sky.

clouds of steam
(my breath)

She walks beside the road,
brown hair specked white.

Her hands, face and ears pink,
half frozen.

She was sad once because
her canary died.

I wonder if she got a new one.

She always got
good grades, she made the
honour roll two times.

The girl had two sisters and a brother.
Lived in a small town in
South-Western Ontario.

Listen, can you hear the soft incense
of her breath burning?

What tragedy or Christ-like experience
shapes her, molds her?

A dog follows her,
licking her dangling hands,
like John or Peter or Judas.

What is it she really wants-
she doesn't understand.
Doesn't understand Joan
of Arc, the martyrs,
the witch burnings,
stolen continents, Montezuma,
Cortes and Pizarro.

The Fifth Baptist

Her manner as elegant
as a cheese grater
raked across the face
and bubble gum thoughts
ooze up from
the shadowy entrails of her mind
and various shades of repression
of the church
of the husband
from the self
swallow up any hint of doubt
Yes, I have the kingdom
you proclaim
and you desperately want to share it
with me, with that other guy
with anyone with two ears
and a short attention span.
You subtly try to nudge your way in
to the place where so many have stood before.
You want to take my hand
and drag me, kicking and screaming
to your version of paradise.
You're not the first.
Won't be the last.
I don't claim to know God better
than any other man,
but all I know is that God is love
and any other idea is murderous addition,
like taking a crayon to a Van Gogh.
I don't begrudge you your faith

but it seems to be too limiting for one so young
at the beginning of things
as if you were keeping one eye
firmly shut on purpose.

The Emperor of Antarctica

John Nash was the
Emperor of Antarctica
but he traded in
his power to command penguins
and his vast dominions
of frozen wastes and
icebergs breaking off
into the Antarctic sea
for a tiny medal
he could wear around
his neck and the
respect of his peers.
He has fled the realm of dreams
and the island of Circe.
And he has shown us
how the greedy devour flesh
canines barred vehement growl
I prefer the sweet, but deadly
strains of the witches jig
the cancer of the mind
to the shore where men eat men
and obscurity-where they
ask you quite gently
not to peek behind the curtain.

The Door Keeper

my father was a janitor
he swept up the refuse
the decaying rinds
he would reach into piles of garbage
and extract things which
would not burn.
He was the stern Christ of Judgment
and stale bread, pop cans and paper bags
were souls shoved in-between
damnation and redemption
and his grimy hand
was clasped to paradise.

Grandpa's Dead

Death, the final close of the door
separates us, and yet cements us.
I do not know what I was,
if anything to you
but I knew you were ready
with a smile and kind word
when nervous I stumbled
through your doors. Maybe
like other men you had your flaws
but they were hidden from me.
I never heard your anger or unkind words.
So I will spare you the false tears
and let the jackals of guilt stalk others
you and I demanded nothing of each other.
Let others carry your body down
to the open arms of the grave
your spirit has already flown
somewhere beyond the imagination.
I will give the best memorial I know
these words and when the time
comes to close my eyes maybe someone
will remember me as I have remembered you.

My Father's Rage

I sit with my recollections
and a bowl of soup
at the bottom of which lies
feta cheese, half melted
and my father's rage.
A rage which lacks a chassis
and a stencil to guide the lead lines.

Both the feta and the rage melt
the feta for a moment:
acrid and vaginal on the tongue
the rage much longer, maybe decades
It is tart, over night coffee.

That rage of coffee tartness
is familiar for me
it has been injected into my veins
it has been moulded to my D.N.A.
it has a long shelf life.

I stretch back to the
comic severity of the Cold,
yet scalding war
I reach out and snatch that rage
I clutch it to my breast
but it is not my child
we are the same age, it and I.

It was conceived with
hawk cop cars and revolvers drawn
it lingered in the womb for three months
with little blue pills, electroshock
with one t.v. channel watching golf
and nurses who told you when to shit.

All through the eighties
the poster of the Incredible Hulk
and the Knight Rider
all through the eighties
wars in El Salvador and Nicaragua
and the Transformers and the Thundercats
to the Berlin Wall falling,
we shared a childhood.

The worm, the shape shifter, the shadow
linger over us like a plague
threatened-through suicidal tendencies
threatened-through social rejection
threatened-through my first kiss,
love, travel and a formal education
threatened to burst like a storm
breaking the uterine walls and
dragging the placenta along with it.

It burst-the last year of school
he ran off for three days
and hitch-hiked to Hamilton.
They gave him stronger medication
and we poured silence, like foam over it.

It burst- we both screaming at
the top of our lungs into the phone
and then the little blue pills,
electroshock,
one t.v. channel watching golf
and nurses who told you when to shit.

"Do you think it's funny?"

"No, Dad, I sob."

My Mother's Rage

you were always the strong one
always brave
with a smile that shrugged off doubt
little did I know the shell was cracking
merciless inch, by merciless inch
you taught me to be good
and now I wonder whether you believe
in good and evil anymore
progressing little step by little step
equating life with survival

the years like centuries
slow, ponderous, elephant's paws
you carried your burden
up and down the slopes of Golgotha

now I don't remember
when your laughter wasn't
mixed with a sigh.

Lines for my Unborn Children

Child, find your place here-
whether it's some place distant
on a ship in the middle of the ocean
battered by the winds and the saline swells
or around a table in a pub
drinking cold beer, and back-slaps
the voices of friends roaring like the sea.
Love who you want, but don't be a slave to that love.
Be loyal, but discard those unworthy of your love.
situations, some ravenous, will confront you.
Some are carnivores, some are paper tigers.
Some want to destroy you. Be stronger.
Know that you are strong, that you can move continents
with a distracted flick of your finger.
Know, too, that weakness sometimes is a strength.
The one who nurses wounds is stronger
than the one who inflicts them.
Be yourself-whatever that self may be.
Fashion is a finicky butterfly.
Those who base their characters on fashion,
are as substantial as those delicate insects.
A flash of colour, and then snuffed out.
Know that you will die, but don't let
this knowledge strangle you.
It is the shade that sharpens the image.
There are a galaxy of things to tell
someone just stepping onto the platform of life
all the books written, or ever written could hardly hold them,
but finally-dream. A person is only as real as their dreams.

Go to Sleep

Go to sleep
little girl, little girl.
Go to sleep
little girl, little girl.
The world's sometimes cold and unfriendly.
Little girl, little girl
But here it's nice and warm and toasty.
Go to sleep
Little girl, little girl.

On the Ides of March

the brunt stench of winter
the pangs
the branches swaying
the soil pounded

jettison
the bravery of birth

tulips push up
the buds
crack open
tendrils exploring

in the slime drenched muck
travel strenuous
footsteps
belch up spring
in the womb swamps
of a season lost.

I would

I would place
a golden statue
in the sunlight
let it burn by glittering
it doesn't matter what
it is
a bird
a scene of war.

For a Friend

The pallid moon
forgives your almond skin
and the sea
the sea laps your sadness.

Twilight

the twilight shimmers
between the serenading walnut leaves
breezes wistfully caress
the gaily clad Mennonite women
working in their village empire.

Triumph

Triumph is another word for loss.
The clay cliffs crack and crumble,
pieces break off and tumble into allegory.
The first view an impatient mistress
the subtle waves toss off prying gulls
the clouds leer, threaten rain.

The Sunset

the sunset
an opulent eden
bursting
the waves lap against the beach
turn it turquoise

Match

a wooden match
that flames up
spurts out
with a whim of smoke—
that's all it is.

Kite

I had a kite
that flew higher and higher
the wind stopped
and it fell
and with it
all the hopes pinned to the tail.

Thunderstorm on the Highway

The rain falls in heaps,
no, it wasn't rain
but the gentle nudging
of the ocean.
We peer through the
dim curtains of wetness
and can decipher nothing.
No hieroglyphics, no yellow and white
lines copulating like snakes on the pavement.
Occasionally a brief taunt of lightning.
Clarity. Then again the stubborn, jarring
embrace of dimness.
Currents of rain piss down
the windshield-windows
flowing with-jagged rhythm-
the highway.

Watchful

The watchful sky delights me
it is not the city sky-
drunk with fog
lit by a few timid flecks
like jacks from a
child's game of marbles
that has been forgotten
or traded for some fresher novelty.
No, this sky-with its boisterous
shivering eyes, is my sky-
and an icicle hangs
from the eaves trough
and I sit in this darkened house
with nothing but winter on my mind.

Snowstorm

There is a moment in the snowstorm
when the universe is ejaculated
and galaxies spin around you
in estrus foetus flakes
copulatory migratory flakes
of ice of sand.

Day, Summer

a cloud swims
the sky a pale infant blue
insects converse
the rudiments of an empire

a tractor orange and white
dragged behind
the plow cracks open
the fertile earth
the gulls float like icebergs
on the black ocean
nervous worms grope like fish
blind and desperate

maple keys
slant downwards
like drunken helicopters

leaf hoppers jump up
the thistles pink purple probe
stinging nettles silent growl

a lad emerges gray
covered in clay
mother mother
it was just my play

turkey vultures orbit
feeding
on rabbits raccoons
unfortunate cats dogs
they met their ends
by murderous headlights

a fox dives into the corn
red and white and black
we last see his bushy tail
parting the sea like
the red sea Moses

the dog and child play
the dog steals the ball
and lies in the shade.

Green Walnut Leaves

the green walnut leaves
clap in the decaying sun
the sound of a dirty lawnmower
transgresses the silence
suburban silence
that whirls around my head.

take these green lips
green from the praying branches
take these black fingers
black from peeling the nuts

press them to your twilight skies
like a lipstick mark on your cheek
like a smudged finger print

the air is calm now, still now
and the war between a man
and his ornamental plants ceases.

new sounds now fill up
the space between silence
and tumult

cars, cars, cars
and the thumping, blaring
stereos of young men.

Night, Winter

welcome to the poverty of night
the dissolute light
embeds itself
in the womb of darkness

the buildings cower
in the absence of light
the blaring store fronts
beacon like polished china
and all the world is glittering

we pass the apathetic beggar
the gaudy tinsel
our lady of the rain
and the world glitters

the dragon clouds
swallow the impervious moon
the leaves tumble
like toppling centuries

there is an old man
with a cigarette
between his lips

there is a buxom girl
shooting pool
hallowed by an electric light
dangling
a waitress comes
with bills held
between her fingers

the table is set
the clinking glasses
and utensils
a candle is burning down
and languid currents
of wax are dripping
along the candle's spine

the straggling hermit star
the dancing breath
fumbling tumbling
the tortoise shell ice
like a babe placenta crowned
the orphan streets
proclaim declaim
the plunge of darkness

the building aroused
throbs up beside the water
the windows
slow electric burn
spew light into the water
it floats threads weaves
it breaks the abstinence
of the night

the ride home on the bus
our cheeks clawed by fluorescence
the squirming writhing bodies
flesh to flesh cheek to glass
closer than sin

the desire come up
then pushed down again
the doors open

the cars thrust by
past Landsdowne
past Morrow Park
and the houses thin-

Peterborough Winter

here in this
ever blowing, ice strangled place
I would like to write of tulips
winged ants mating
semen stroked and finished
but the season is a barbiturate

the trees shiver
the lank limpid streets
at absolute zero
I would like to break
the fasting winter
but the chill has frozen my cells.

sometimes in the south
the pocked-marked moon becomes orange
and katydids act out Don Giovanni
to be born and mate and die
all in three days

I've moved north a couple of latitudes.

Coffee

I remember
we met for coffee
on remembrance day
the banners were flapping
red and white
the red autumn leaves
the white flecks of snow.

Painter

If I were a painter
vivid colours would drip from my brush
and I would carve the
lines so delicately
you would touch the fames
of the sunset and burn your fingers.

I would roll my eyes like dice
against the infant glaciers and coal mountains
and lock what I saw on cattle skin.

The ocean is fat
and the mountains on the coast
sit light upon it.

Mosquitoes

mosquitoes
circum
navigate
my head
three willow
trees branches
trimmed just
beyond kid
high
a single
bird
chirps
and I remember my grandfather's willow tree
with luxuriant branches
and we would swing
like Tarzan, from one end
of the meadow to the other.

Outburst

outburst and roaring
the jet gallops and lifts
up through the layer of smog
and the green toy world drops away.

In Preston

ducks laughing
leaf swims under
The gray dimpling
water

my tram

the tram
runs off lunges
quick and swift steel rattles
I sit, unsure if this is it
my tram.

View

The half moon-yellow
seen through the light pink gauze
of the ill patterned curtain
above the firm line
of a block of flats.

Deer

deer and storks
hop through the rye field
glanced briefly.

Sparrow

sparrow flies
thin pines brood and pivot
quick escape.

Pines

the brooding pines
scratch at the tattered curtain of the sky
as if it were a human thing
and could bleed.

Boar

the light slants
through the trees
shadow on shadow
intertwine and still
the diligent spiders
weave away
too early for human eyes
or proverbs-

the webs shatter
the light
hung with care
between
the strong femurs
of grinding pines

and somewhere
deep in the dark bush
a wild boar
grunts and squeaks.

Babel

a dog barks
a rooster crows
rain drops erratic rhythm
then sudden burst
and then all is silent
for a few pregnant seconds

Spring's Sleeping

What causes the spring
to wake in fits
like the restless sleep of a drunk man?
The dogs barking in heat
the birds-winging exhausted to roost?
No. It is the old woman
stooped over, wearing slippers,
sweeping the dirt with a too short brush,
muttering curses under her breath
She has disturbed Spring's sleeping.

Snow is Better

Snow is better than rain.
It falls gently on the window pane
like a mother's embrace.

Rain On Bialogora

the descant of the birds
the solemn stammer of the mountain
the trees rise up
like shivering hairs.

the Baltic mumbles
half dirge, half complaint,
the first death by brine.

I could live here, eat blue berries
confess my sins to the envious trees
grow fat and lazy
and pretend to be wise.

On the Bus to Montreal

I'm looking
for a word
that doesn't exist
something in green
with garlands of pine cedar
other winter trees
here where summer
is an old man
hobbling towards
his final plummet
the long slithering road
between Ottawa and Montreal
rises up to meet us
like a cold
or a joyful and courageous
snake
we head east
sunrise
east
on the bus to
Montreal.

Alberta

Are there any poets in Alberta
I wonder as I recall
the violent imagery of the place
that streams bleeds into your vision
mountain. Stop. Glacier. Stop.
Plummet. Stop.

It seems to me that all
the poets here are tourists
with their clicking shutters
of ink and apertures of paper
but they possess the luxury of flight.

The land scares the writers
here to prose.
The mountains are bullies,
but subtle as well.
They taunt:
reduce me to verse
to simile, to metaphor.

A mountain is an impassive sea:
a lust of topography.

The flat lander can not conceive the mountain
but with impotent adjectives like
majestic-awe-serene.

But the mountain confronts me
with exploding verbs
aching-heavy-throbbing

the mountain is an enigma
stillness which betrays movement.

Alberta is an infested word,
it is no longer the moniker
of a long dead princess,
it is infected with grizzlies
pine resin and granite.

Epitaph: Alberta
not a place
but a
carnivore.

Eden Drive, North Vancouver

I ask her if she
wants to go for a walk
and she says, 'sure, where to?'
to which I say, 'the mountain'.

We leave the hotel beginning
to eat our supper of bread
stuffed with cream cheese
or the other option,
of peanut butter, and follow
the winding paths into the
forest. They all seem to lead
to the river.

So we go up from the forest
and into the city. We head
for a bunch of houses on a hill.
As we begin our ascent I notice
palm bushes, ivy and holly.

Everything here seems to have
been bought. From the volvos to the flora and fauna.
The view of the harbour is marvelous,
although I suspect that it was purchased, too.

Every so often in this neighbourhood,
where there are no sidewalks
or no one who seems out of place
(someone working or paying someone to)
there's signs saying: Warning.
Suspicious behaviour will be reported
to the police.

I wondered what would be
considered suspicious in this
neighbourhood of rich white-people.
Profanity? The wrong colour of skin?
A nipple ring?

An elderly gentleman looks at my clothes
and says good afternoon so insincerely
it grates my nerves. Again, banished
from Eden. Where's my fucking
apple?

Poppies

Look at the ground and your feet walking on it
and know someone died here
for something they believed in or didn't.
There's poppies on the road from Villanubla to Valladolid
from the bones of the victims of the crusade
or in other places of the revolution
but the blood was the same colour,
the colour of poppies bobbing
up and down in the wind.

Snow in Dal-Dong-Ju-Gong

there's a blanket of snow
that covers the dirty city streets
like a shroud of joy
like something clean
and the good people of Ulsan
gawk at it, prod it
throw it up into the air
and see it as an immense obstacle
that bars their progress, but with
tiny joyful smiles on their faces.

The Hermit Kingdom

I am locked
in this jewel encrusted
genies' bottle.
I forage in the shards of glass
like a grazing goldfish.
Music drifts up
to my window
from the Rocky Restaurant
and the Victoria buffet
and the dull roar of traffic
is like the sea
which breaks in
limitless cycles
across the pockmarked rocks
and the arrogant sound
of the tv rumbles
in the other room.
This is Korea.
It seems a bit removed
from the Shilla and the
breast shaped burial mounds
and the celestial horses
kicking up the sod of the sky.

Fern

I am sitting in my darkened and darkening room
my only companion a nervous fern
thinking of happier or more purposeful times
when I stirred up the dust of the future
with imaginary steps.
And now real dust settles into
the corners of my neglected room
where I have slept as a sojourner.
I will leave this place and the next
and they and I will fade from memory.
I am as permanent as my name
written into the sand at Bialogora;
as permanent as forgotten poems
abandoned in closets in Peterborough
as permanent as two rings
plop-plopped into the Taewa.

Walking on Bones

I walk on bones
of Jews massacred silently,
angrily, with smiles on
the culprits' faces
and a shot of vodka, after
by the fireplace, legs kicked up
and a bear rug
Jews ratted on by neighbours
scared to walk the street
denounced by little girls
with Aryan ringlets
Jews stuffed, suffocating in closets,
crawl spaces, bricked up rooms
ghetto Jews, defiant Jews
turncoat Jews of the JP the judenrat
little boys hiding the forests
scared to, and forgetting how
to speak. Their ghosts
dance in the wind
like the white, pure flecks of snow
like grey flecks of ash.

Grandma's New Face

frost etched
like the veins of a leaf
on the window
of the tram stop shelter
an incoherent crone
with varicose veins like tapeworms
and liver spots
and a dab of foundation
on her over sized nose
begs for 20 grosz
spring birds sing
yellow morning clouds
saunter off + the tram comes
the lady endures +me off to work

Slap on the back

old ladies wait to buy bread
young boys spray graffiti on walls
that says 'fucking kike' in red
buddies, slap on the back and big balls.

www.ingramcontent.com/pod-product-compliance
Ingram Content Group UK Ltd.
Pitfield, Milton Keynes, MK11 3LW, UK
UKHW022025190726
13853UKWH00005B/2114